THE BLACK IS BEAUTIFUL
BEAUTY BOOK

BY MELBA MILLER

THE BLACK IS BEAUTIFUL BEAUTY BOOK

Illustrated by LORENZO

Prentice-Hall, Inc. Englewood Cliffs,
New Jersey

Printed in the United States of America ·J

Prentice-Hall International, Inc., London
Prentice-Hall of Australia, Pty. Ltd., North Sydney
Prentice-Hall of Canada, Ltd., Toronto
Prentice-Hall of India Private Ltd., New Delhi
Prentice-Hall of Japan, Inc., Tokyo

Library of Congress Cataloging in Publication
Data

Miller, Melba.
  The Black is beautiful beauty book.

  SUMMARY: Advice to black girls on basic
health, exercise, cosmetics, and the care of teeth
and hair.
  1. Women, Negro—Health and hygiene—Ju-
venile literature. [1. Beauty, Personal. 2.
Hygiene] I. Lynch, Lorenzo, 1932– illus. II.
Title.
RA778.M63   613'.04'243   73-20170
ISBN 0-13-077388-3

10   9   8   7   6   5   4   3

TABLE
OF
CONTENTS

CHAPTER 1
Your Skin

1

Skin is something most of us pretty much take for granted. It's important to remember, however, that how your skin will look and act later depends on how well you treat it now. Good skin care is essential to looking your best, and keeping skin clean and healthy is the first step.

Our skin performs some very important jobs for us. First of all, it holds our bodies together and keeps our insides in place. It protects them from the elements and keeps out most dirt and germs. It acts as a thermostat to keep our bodies at an even temperature and gets rid of excess waste in the form of perspiration. It sends up oil to help keep itself lubricated and can even replace itself when injured. Now, for all the wonderful things our skin does for us, we must give it plenty of attention and care so it can always do its best. Let's start at the top with our face.

All facial skin is not the same. The three basic types are oily, dry and normal.

It's easy to tell oily skin. The pores are large and the skin is shiny. Oily skin tends to get pimples and blemishes, but it doesn't dry out as much as drier skin and it gets less oily as you grow older. While you're waiting for it to improve, though, keep it clean. There are soaps made just for oily skin. They dry out excess oils and help keep your face feeling clean and nice. If your hair is dirty the excess oils will mix with the oils of your face and aggrevate blemishes. Wash your hair often. It really will help keep your skin clear.

Although everybody who has oily skin doesn't necessarily have acne, it poses a special problem for the person with oily skin. Certain hormones have the job of telling the oil-producing glands when to send oil as well as how much to keep your skin soft and smooth. But when a girl is around twelve years of age, these messages start getting confused and the glands wind up overproducing and clogging pores with too much oil. When the pores are clogged with oil, your face becomes a sitting duck for all kinds of bacteria that combine with the oils to cause acne. In bad cases, the pimples will fill with pus and become inflamed. It's because of these inflamed pimples that there are scars and pits long after the acne has gone.

Since acne can really damage your skin, it's best to see a doctor as soon as you can. In the meantime, KEEP YOUR FACE CLEAN! Washing won't cure acne, but it certainly helps control oil buildup. It only takes a couple of hours for oil to build up and clog a pore, so keep your face clean. Use a drying soap and scrub for at least two full minutes. Rinse well and scrub again. Use your hands (make sure they're clean!) to wash your face. Wash cloths and brushes won't do the trick because they carry germs that you just don't need.

While washing your face, massage it, too. Use circular motions that go up and out. This is good for firming up the muscles in your face. When you finish washing, pat your face dry with a towel and apply an astringent. When you have acne, your face needs to dry out and the old skin must peel off. Make sure you get an astringent that isn't too harsh. Harsh ones can remove too much oil, causing

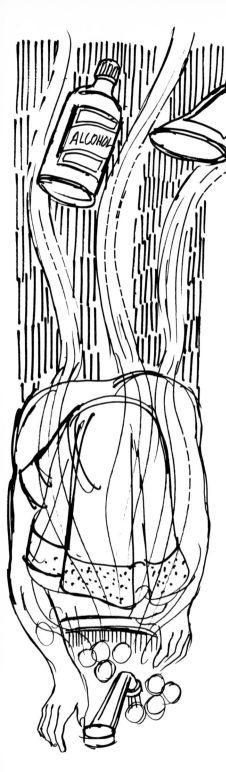

your oil glands to overproduce, thus creating a worse oil problem than you had in the first place. Mild astringents can be found in any drugstore or you can make them yourself. Mix a pint of alcohol, a drop of oil (baby oil will do), and a drop or two of perfume. It's cheap and works just fine. Apply the astringent with a cotton ball all over your face after you wash.

You might want to give yourself a facial sauna to open up clogged pores. You can use plain water or you can add herbs like camomile, rosemary and basil which are available on the spice shelf at grocery stores. Put water into a pot and boil. Once it is boiling, add the herbs and turn off the stove. Drape a towel over your head and the pot so none of the steam will escape. Hold your face over the steam until the steam stops. If you prefer, you can heat the water in a kettle and then pour it in a face bowl. If the water from your tap gets really hot, plug up your face bowl and steam your face there. Afterwards, apply an astringent.

If you have acne, there are a few basic things you should keep in mind:

Watch what you eat

Greasy foods, sodas and sweets don't help, either. Also, you might have an allergy, so avoid rich foods that are known to be irritating like chocolate, nuts, shellfish. Eat lots of fresh fruits and vegetables and drink plenty of water. Water flushes the waste out of your body which can also affect your skin.

Try not to get uptight

Stay away from cleansing creams and heavy moisturizers

Since your skin needs to dry out, these will only add to the problem of too much oil. If

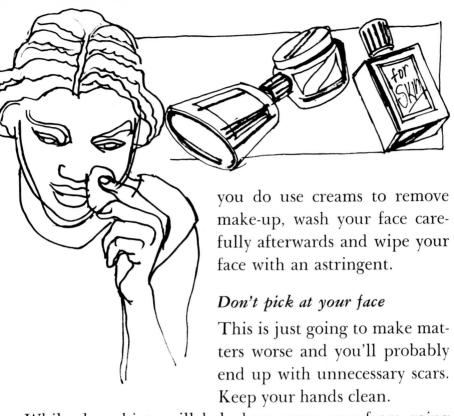

you do use creams to remove make-up, wash your face carefully afterwards and wipe your face with an astringent.

Don't pick at your face

This is just going to make matters worse and you'll probably end up with unnecessary scars. Keep your hands clean.

While these hints will help keep your acne from going wild, only a doctor can cure it. Try to see one as soon as the problem starts.

Most black women have dry skin. The skin looks rough and flaky and feels tight on your face. Other problem areas are knees, elbows and feet. When it comes to the care of dry skin, moisturizing is the key. Every day our skin loses some of its natural moisture because of weather and the environment. It's necessary to replace this moisture to keep skin smooth and soft. Use moisturizing soaps or cream cleansers to clean your face. Just smooth a little on your face, massage for a few seconds and tissue off. Since most women suffer from dry skin, you will find an endless array of products to help fight it. Moisturizers are included in some foundations, eye shadows, blushers and lipsticks. You'll find moisturizers to wash with or apply afterwards, under-make-up moisturizers and moisturizers to soften your skin while you sleep. The main differences between these various products are in when and how they are applied.

Because dry skin shows up so well on us, black people have always been into using lots of oils and lotions. To avoid ashy skin, we've been applying lubricants from head to toe all our lives. As a result, we've learned that using lotion is also an easy way to smell nice. When times get tough, however, even Vaseline will get the job done. Black women didn't have time to get caught up in names and claims; grease was grease and all served the purpose. In fact, whatever was used worked so well, it was assumed that black skin was oilier than white skin. We have always known that our skin tends to be dry. Now we've got the rest of the world running around trying to recapture lost youth and young skin and spending fortunes doing it. All this is to say that whatever you use is up to you. Don't think that if you don't use an expensive cream your skin will dry up like a raisin. Whatever moisturizer you choose, make sure you use it every day. It's a good idea to

apply cream or lotion right after you wash your face, to restore the protection of oil.

Winter is the enemy of dry skin. As cold weather sets in, you need to give your face extra protection. Never go out without first putting on a protective cream or lotion. Too much sun can also cause dry skin to dry out further. Be sure to use a moisturizer before and after spending time in the sun.

Normal skin has just the right amount of oil, enough to protect you from the climate and not enough to become a problem. Even so, normal skin requires the same amount of care as dry or oily skin in order to maintain its balance. Use a cream for makeup removal and apply a *mild* lotion after washing to tighten pores. Never use a harsh astringent. It can cause normal skin to dry out in no time. And be sure to protect your skin from any severe weather conditions. A moisturizer is a good idea if you plan to be outdoors in wind or sun. Plenty of fresh air, exercise, good diet and enough sleep will help keep your face balanced and fresh.

Some people with normal skin have a few oily patches on their faces, usually on the forehead and around the nose. If you have this problem, treat your face as though you have normal skin, and use a slightly stronger astringent on the oily areas only. This will help to clear up the problem without drying out the rest of your face.

Along with creams and cleansers, facial masques and steam are beneficial for all kinds of skin. They help unclog pores and loosen dead skin cells. Masques, which come in a variety of types, can be bought to suit your own skin's needs. There are clay masques which dry out the skin and so are excellent for oily skins. Peel-off masques are available, too. They are good for oily and normal skins. There are also masques that you massage off. These are especially good for people with acne because they dry the skin out and flake off dead cells.

For dry skin there are moisturizing masques. You can also give yourself a sauna in the same way that was described for oily skin. But instead of water use oil and apply a moisturizer afterwards.

When summer comes, protect your face against the harshness of the sun. Remember, black people *do* sunburn. Use a sun "screen," cream that shuts out the sun's harmful rays. If you have acne, summer will usually bring improvement because of the drying and peeling effects the sun provides. But don't overdo it. Sun is good for your skin, but only when you take it in moderation. A bad sunburn can cause skin to dry out and become leathery, making your skin look old when you're still young.

When we were little girls our mothers took care of our bodies. We didn't have to worry about baths, and body odor had not yet become a big problem. As we get older, though, taking care of our bodies becomes our responsibility. Just as your mother doesn't dress you anymore, she shouldn't have to tell you when to bathe, either.

Your skin perspires to cool itself off. This activity goes on winter and summer alike. Perspiration alone is practically odorless, but when it combines with bacteria on your skin odor results. Take care of your body as you take care of your face. Wash it every day. You wouldn't think of leaving the house in the morning before you wash your face and brush your teeth, right? Well, feel the same way about the rest of yourself. Use a deodorant every day. Deodorants reduce the amount of bacteria on your skin and so prevent odor. Antiperspirants do, too, plus they contain a chemical to stop you from perspiring as much as you ordinarily would. Both deodorants and antiperspirants work best on clean skin. Which kind you choose is up to you. If you hate to feel wet under the arms, use an antiperspirant. But remember, nothing is going to stop you from perspiring altogether. It's a necessary bodily function.

Underarm hair traps sweat and stops deodorant from getting to the skin. This means there's a greater chance for odor. Removing the hair is your best bet. You can do it by shaving or with a cream hair remover called a depilatory. If you choose a depilatory, be sure to follow instructions. It's entirely a matter of personal choice, but if you do decide to shave your underarms, remember that it is something that must be done regularly and often. Shaved areas become stubbly very quickly. Don't decide you must shave simply because "everyone is doing it." They're not. It's a decision that's hard to reverse, since growing hair back looks messy in the process. Think about it first—you may decide that removing stubble every few days is simply not worth it.

If you do decide to remove underarm hair, you can either shave or use a hair removing cream called a depilatory. Electric razors and conventional safety razors both work well. A cream depilatory produces the same results as a razor, and using one or the other is a matter of preference. A depilatory, however, can irritate sensitive skin, so follow the directions on the package and switch to a razor if your skin becomes irritated. It's also a good idea to apply a soothing moisturizer after using a depilatory.

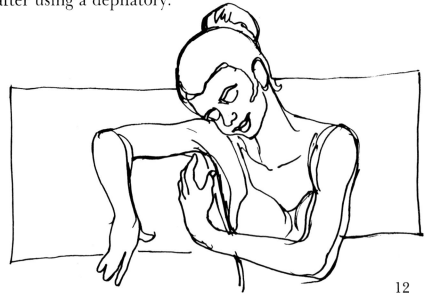

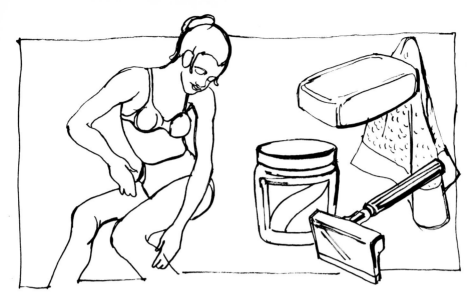

Removing leg hair is also a personal choice. Again, if you decide to remove it, either a razor or a depilatory can be used. Since the skin on your legs is generally less sensitive than the skin under your arms, a depilatory is less likely to irritate your legs.

Besides keeping ourselves clean and odor-free, we have to take care of our skin. There are lots of things to help skin and a bath is a fun way to do it.

For moisturizing your skin while you bathe, there are bath oils, beads, milk baths and gels. Milk baths make you feel soft and silky but not greasy as some oils do. Gels clean you while you soak and are great for tender skin. Then there are bath salts and crystals that soften water so soap will lather easily. They're fun, too, since they smell wonderful and turn your bath different colors. Bubble bath also softens water.

There are great things to be found right around the house that will help dry skin. Oatmeal is one. Put some oatmeal in an old stocking and swish it around in the bath water until it gets cloudy. Baking soda, too, will soften water and help your skin. If you exercised too much and your muscles ache, Epsom salt will relax them and relieve soreness. And many doctors maintain that vegetable oil or shortening is the best moisturizer for dry skin.

There are problem areas that need extra care like knees, ankles and elbows. While bath moisturizers help, you also need extra tools to remove dead skin. A pumice stone, found at the drugstore, removes dead skin when rubbed on heels, knees, elbows, ankles and soles. Used every day, it will keep these trouble spots nice and soft. Loofahs, which are rough, natural sponges, come either packaged in squares like a bath cloth or long (about a foot and a half) and round for hard-to-reach places. They'll remove dead skin you didn't know you had and make you feel all nice and tingly. Soap it and use it instead of a bath cloth. There are long-handled brushes that stimulate and also get to those hard-to-reach spots. Creams are available to remove dead skin and soften rough spots. The difference between them and regular lotions and moisturizing creams is that they contain ingredients that act like a pumice

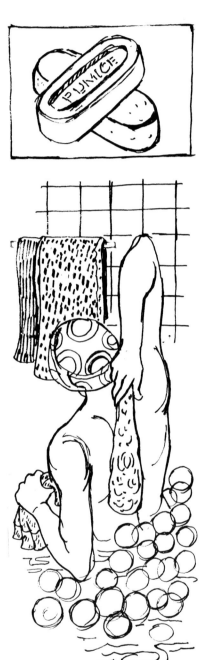

14

stone. As you rub the cream into your heels, for instance, it begins to feel a little gritty and you'll find the dead skin rubbing off. Used every day, it will make those rough spots soft and smooth.

When you take a bath or shower, don't make the water too hot. Very hot water dries your skin. On the other hand, a warm bath will relax you, a cold to lukewarm one will pick you up. When you finish, pat yourself dry and apply lotion right away. Rub it in all over while the skin is still slightly damp for more moisturizing action. There are also bath oil sprays that smell good for after the bath and friction lotions to cool you and make your skin tingle. For extra dry skin, apply lotion or oil *before* the bath as well as after. This is a good idea for showers, too.

You can do lots of nice things for yourself during your bath besides getting clean. Get in the habit of making your bath a very special time. Collect all the things you need before you start. You can give yourself a facial (the masque kind) while you're in the tub. Rubber trays that fit across the bathtub come in very handy for holding things. Another thing you can do is chill some cotton balls in equal parts of rosewater and witch hazel before your bath. When you're in the tub, close your eyes and put the dampened balls on your lids. Lie back and think good thoughts.

A bath can make you forget how rotten you feel or how bad the day was. It can make you feel pretty and pampered. You can clean and moisturize your body, relax your muscles, soothe your mind and just get away from it all.

CHAPTER 2
Your Face

2

Have you ever found yourself staring into the mirror, wishing you had your best friend's eyes, your cousin's dimples or even the pretty smile of that girl in your English class whom you really can't stand? I guess we all, at some time or another, daydream about that one thing we need to make us absolutely satisfied and beautiful to boot.

It doesn't take long to discover that however long you pinch your nose, it's not going to change its shape. There are things you can do, though, to bring out your good points and play down the not-so-good ones.

Go back to your mirror and take a good long look. If you decide you don't look like whoever you happen to think is the most beautiful girl in the world, cheer up! Chances are, whoever she is, she had to develop her beauty. Very few women who are considered beauties were born that way. They just learned how to bring out their good features. You can, too.

Smile. Your teeth are a good place to begin. They occupy a pretty important spot on your face—your mouth. And if your mouth is not together, your face won't be, either. Good dental habits should start at an early age, but if yours didn't, it's still not too late. Start right now.

Every time you eat, tiny pieces of food stay between your teeth. Even when you can't see them, they're there. When these food particles aren't removed, they combine with bacteria and turn into soft, gooey plaque. Plaque can be removed with a toothbrush and dental floss. If you don't remove it, it will turn into a very hard substance called tartar. Tartar must be scraped off by a dentist. If it isn't, it can cause cavities and gum disease and eventually make you lose your teeth. Few people realize how important healthy gums are. Remember, they help hold your teeth in place and they can begin to recede rapidly if not taken care of properly. By doing some very simple things which only take a few minutes, however, you can prevent tartar from forming.

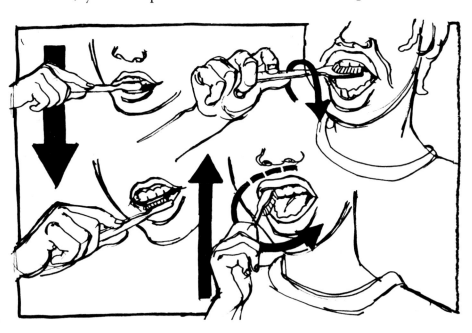

Buy some dental floss. Floss and brush after every meal. Break off a piece of floss long enough to handle with both hands and clean all the spaces between your teeth. After flossing, brush up and down making sure you get every single surface, inside and out. Whatever you miss will tell on you because that's where tartar will form. Flossing may seem like a chore, especially since you can't always see the results immediately. But you'll feel the results over a long period of time when your mouth stays healthy, so spend some time on your teeth. Don't just give them the once-over.

See your dentist regularly. Don't wait for a toothache to drive you there. With regular visits, you can avoid trouble before it begins. You should see your dentist twice a year.

With so many products on the market these days, it's hard to decide between all the brighteners and whiteners and fluorides and polishes. What we need is an order of importance in caring for our teeth. The most important thing is making sure you keep them. Cavities and gum disease cause many people to lose their teeth. Fluoride fights cavities. Combined with regular brushing and flossing, it will make for both healthy teeth and healthy gums. Some areas have fluoride in their water, but just to be sure, use a toothpaste which contains it. As for the brighteners and whiteners, many of them can do real damage to your teeth. They contain chemicals that are much too harsh on the tooth enamel and can actually scratch it. It's important that the enamel be strong and damage-free since that's what the outer coating of your teeth is made of. Besides, strong, healthy teeth are not necessarily white teeth. It's a better idea to avoid the things that make healthy teeth dingy like coffee, tea and especially cigarettes.

Mouthwashes are nice but, if you are taking care of your teeth and gums, unnecessary. If you aren't taking good care of your mouth, mouthwashes won't do the trick. That doesn't mean we don't sometimes need to freshen our breath. For a good natural mouthwash, chew a sprig of parsley and rinse with salt water. Sucking on a whole clove is even simpler.

If you're thinking about waterpicks, they're great for stimulating the gums, which is important, but they can't take the place of flossing and brushing after every meal.

Finally, again watch what you eat. Your diet has a lot to do with the shape your teeth are in. Naturally, candy is not the best thing in the world for your teeth. Sweets will tear away at your teeth quicker than anything else. On the other hand, chewing on raw carrots and celery is great for them. It even helps remove some of the food particles that get lodged between your teeth and send you searching for a toothpick. (Speaking of toothpicks, they can do damage to your gums.)

Once you get all your teeth, they'll be the only ones you have. Sure, there are always dentures and plates, but they are expensive and never as functional or comfortable as your natural teeth, and a good program of oral hygiene can prevent the loss of teeth. Besides the health aspect of it—rotten teeth can make you sick all over—a nice smile is the start of being beautiful.

Now that the inside of your mouth is fresh and healthy, let's look at the outside of your mouth—your lips—and the rest of your face. Makeup is one of the fun parts of taking care of yourself. With it, you can change your appearance to highlight your good points and play down your bad ones, or change your face a bit to suit your mood. There's an endless variety of things to do with makeup. You are limited only by your imagination. And a little makeup can go a long way.

Look at yourself. Would you like your eyes to look larger? Maybe you would like to emphasize your cheekbones. Or perhaps you just want to add a little color and glow. Whatever it is, start with a positive attitude. Decide what your best features are and like them. From there you can learn to emphasize those good points and play down the not-so-good.

There are an endless number of products to choose from for just your face alone. You can really do whatever you want to once you have the basics down. Some people don't consider themselves made up unless they have on a foundation, blusher, highlights, shadows, liner, mascara, lipstick and a see-through powder to finish everything off. Then there are some who wear eye shadow and mascara and that's all. There are women who don't wear make-up at all. It's really a matter of personal choice. Today, the most popular look is the natural one. That goes for hair and dress as well as for makeup. Most of the ads and commercials place some emphasis on looking natural and healthy. So, while it's fun to try new kinds of makeup and different ways of wearing it, always let what you wear reflect your personality, style and taste.

Since makeup is a general word for many things, let's discuss each one, one by one, in order of application. Keep in mind that fresh makeup works best on fresh skin, so wash carefully first. If you have dry skin, be sure to use a moisturizer first, or a mild astringent if your skin is oily.

Foundations

Sometimes called base, it is the first thing you put on (if you wear it) after moisturizer. When choosing a make-up base, try to get as close to your own skin tone as you can. Today, black women enjoy a whole array of products made especially for our complexions, so finding a shade to match is no problem. Foundations are not supposed to show. They are to give your face an even, smooth look; but still, your face should not look as if it's painted. Foundations come in:

pancake — very thick, used mostly for stage make-up

cream — not as thick, generally gives a dull (matte) finish, but is now available in translucent

liquid — the thinnest and the easiest to blend. Comes in matte or shiny

cover-up stick — for covering a single blemish, used for "on the spot repair"

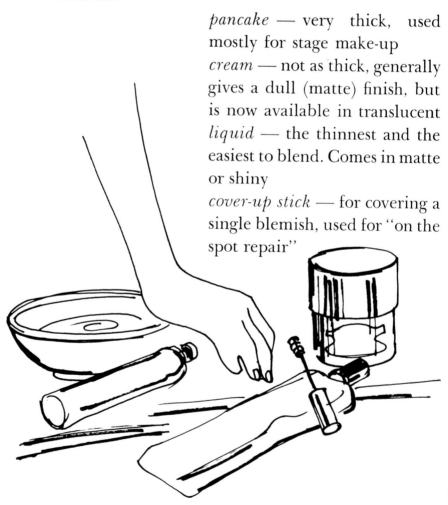

Blushers

Blushers should complement your color. They come in shades from deep pinks to rich bronzes. They too should be blended in well so the healthy glow they provide looks natural. Blushers do the job of highlighting and shading and can be applied to the cheekbones, the hollows or even the forehead. They come in:

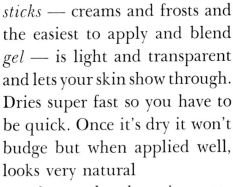

sticks — creams and frosts and the easiest to apply and blend
gel — is light and transparent and lets your skin show through. Dries super fast so you have to be quick. Once it's dry it won't budge but when applied well, looks very natural
powders — brush-on in matte or frosted. Good for shading but not too easy to blend in

Blushers are a good makeup basic. They can be worn without a foundation and when blended in well, make for a nice look.

Eye shadows

With eyes and color, anything goes! Eye shadows come in every color you can think of and even some you can't. Can make large eyes look smaller or small eyes look large. Eye shadows come in:

brush-on powder — matte or frosted and stays on pretty well
cream—also in matte or frosted,

tends to collect in fold of eyelid
if skin is oily or the day is a long
one

crayons — the newest addition
to the shadow family, crayons
are fun and can be used to highlight other parts of the face. Also
come in cream or frosted

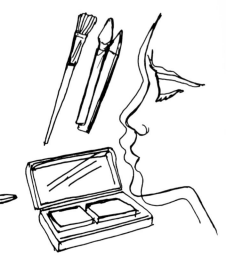

Eye liners

Eye liner is used to emphasize the eye in much the
same way as mascara. It's applied from the inner
corner to the outer corner of the eyelid, very close
to the lashes. Eye liner comes in colors to match
your hair or in pastels and frosteds. All are applied
with a thin brush and require a steady hand. If you
like liner, get one for your hair color and a pastel,
too, for special effects. For instance, if you want your
eyes to look larger, you would line them with something light and shimmery. To make them smaller,
you would use a darker color. Eye liners come in:

cake—applied with a wet brush
and available in only matte hair
colors

liquid—available in pastels and
frosted shades as well as hair
tones, is applied with brush
dipped in the liquid

automatic — only difference is
that the brush always has liner
on it

26

Eyebrow pencil

Is used to even out the eyebrow and can also be used to line the lid. It comes in colors to match the brow's hair.

powder—brush-on powder offers a softer line
pencil—offers a harder line and is best for light brows

Mascara

Mascara highlights eyes by coloring, thickening and lengthening lashes. It comes in hair colors as well as blues, greens, etc. Some have tiny fibers that attach themselves to the ends of your lashes for added length. Mascara is available in:

cake—brush must be dipped in water first
liquid — brush is dipped directly into liquid and then brushed on to lashes with long, even strokes
automatic — less economical than the liquid, automatic mascara has a brush evenly coated with mascara

Lipsticks and glosses

Lipstick colors your lips and comes in tubes, automatic brushes with lipstick that flows out and pots of color that you put on with a brush or your finger. It can be creamy or frosted. If you're going to wear lipstick, get a good start by learning to apply it with a brush. You'll get a better line and a more professional look. Lip brushes are inexpensive and last a long time. One with a sable tip is best. Lipstick, like eye makeup, can change size and shape. You can make your lips appear fuller by highlighting the center of the mouth. That's done by coloring the outer edges of your mouth while putting little or no lipstick in the center. Then gloss over the whole thing. Glosses are mostly for shine and can be worn over lipstick, under it or alone.

A touch of lipstick can be used as a blusher.

Powders

Powders can be loose (like dusting powder) or pressed (like a compact). They're used to finish off a completely made-up face or applied to the nose and forehead to take away shine. Now they're available in translucent—which lets everything you've done to your face show through while pulling the whole thing together.

Before you apply any makeup, have your face in order: Clean teeth, clean skin and well-groomed eyes. Get into the habit of keeping your eyebrows neat. Pluck any hairs that grow between your eyes with tweezers. If your eyebrows themselves need a little shaping, always pluck from beneath the brow instead of on top. This will assure you of following the natural line your eyebrows make. If you wet a face cloth in hot water and place it on your eyebrows, the heat will help loosen the hairs and there won't be much discomfort. If you

massage your eyebrows with a little lotion as well, it will be
even easier. Buy an extra toothbrush to use on your eyebrows. Brushing them up, then from the inside out will improve their appearance and encourage them to grow right.
Never use a razor on your face.

A word about allergies. Some skin is extra-sensitive to
things like wool or detergents or even perfume. Sometimes
you don't know you're allergic to something until you try it.
There are whole groups of things that many people are allergic to. Perfume, wool, tomatoes and chocolate, for example,
are considered to be known allergins. That is, they have a
history of causing allergies in lots of people. Sometimes
makeup will cause swelling and itching. That's because lots
of makeup contains known allergins. There are companies
that take the known allergins, like perfume, out of their
cosmetics. This makeup is said to be hypo-allergenic. Just
because the known allergins have been removed doesn't
mean that it's impossible for anyone to be allergic to it. It
does, though, decrease the chances. If anything you use on

your skin starts to burn or itch or swell, wash it off immediately. Don't use anything that gives you a reaction. If you know already that you are sensitive, you should use the hypoallergenic cosmetics. Most of the bigger companies are taking the cue and are coming out with products labeled hypoallergenic. So there won't be any problem finding what you want.

When you're ready to begin, wash your face so it's super clean. It's no good to pile make-up on a dirty face or one that already has makeup on it. That will only clog pores and we already know that clogged pores are no good. After washing, apply a moisturizer. When you put moisturizer on your face, don't forget your neck as well. Thin skin dries out fast.

Apply foundation

DOT it on your forehead, temples, cheeks, chin, nose, etc., and don't forget your throat and ears.

BLEND it in carefully so it will be perfectly even and natural-looking. Use your fingers or a small sponge.

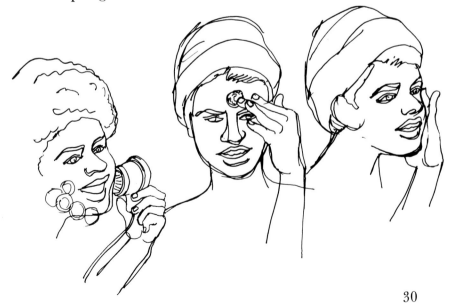

Blush is next

> STREAK it lightly along cheekbones going up towards temples.
>
> BLEND in well over entire cheekbone area.

Now for the shadow

> SMOOTH on entire upper eyelid area from lash line to crease.

Line if you want

> STRETCH eyelid at outer corner (makes lid smoother and line is easier to draw on a smooth lid). DRAW line as close to lashes as possible from inner corner to outer corner. Stop when your lashes do. Bottom lid may also be lined but line must be super thin and again, very close to lashes.

Mascara to top it off

> BRUSH the lashes from underneath using long, even strokes to the tips of the lashes. The more coats

you use, the thicker they will appear. If you use more than one coat, let the first one dry for a couple of minutes before adding more. Putting mascara on the lower lashes can be tricky. They should be brushed from underneath, too, but if your lashes are too short or curly you can dip the brush in the mascara and carefully run the tip over the edges of your bottom lashes. This will color them. Use the toothbrush to separate them. Don't leave any mascara on your lower lids or you'll look like Dracula's wife.

Lips are last

LINE your mouth first. Put some lipstick on the tip of the brush. Start at the outside of your mouth and follow the line in to center. Repeat for the other side. The bottom is done just like the top: outside to center.

FILL in the lines with color using your brush. Lips may also be lined with an eyebrow pencil in a color just slightly darker than the lipstick to be used.

Lips need lots of care and attention. Carefully cream off lipstick at night and apply moisturizer before you go to sleep. Always put a gloss or something on them when you're going outside. Most chapsticks have camphor in them that can dry the lips out. Vaseline is better. Try not to lick your lips because that also dries them out and causes chapping.

Every face has different makeup needs. Once you feel comfortable handling the basic makeup techniques above, it is time to experiment a little, to learn how to play up your good features and play down your bad ones. A lot can be done with a few small tricks. Most of the effects can be adapted to your own needs. You may be awkward at first,

but don't get discouraged. A little practice will solve everything. And once you become adept, nothing will seem easier. One caution, however: Don't overdo! You may not like your nose or your cheekbones, but they're a part of you and looking natural is the key to good makeup.

It's not necessary to put on everything I've mentioned here. Find your own thing and don't be afraid to experiment. Whatever you choose, though, make sure you spend as much time taking it off as you did putting it on. You can use cold creams for dry skin or cleansing lotions for oily skin to gently remove makeup. Put cream all over your face and neck. Massage gently to lift makeup off. For eyelashes you can use baby oil on a cotton ball. There are oils on the market just to remove eye makeup. When you dab the oil on the lashes and around the eye, leave it on for a few minutes. Gently tissue the makeup off eyes and face. Wash your face as usual, depending on your skin type. Apply moisturizer or astringent.

No matter what kind of skin you have, you must keep it clean. Cleanse it in the morning, before you go out in the evening and at bedtime.

Makeup is fun but try not to get too dependent on it. It can bring out your nice features and that's what it's all about. Enhancing the nice things you already have going for you. Finding the right look for yourself takes time and energy but it's well worth the effort. Just don't neglect the basics. Beauty begins with healthy teeth and skin.

Don't worry if you can't seem to get the hang of applying makeup right away. It can take years to be able to master the art. Have a good time experimenting!

* * *

Facial hair can really be a problem. Many women do have it and there are a few things you can do about it. If it doesn't bother you, though, leave it alone. But if it does you can either bleach it or remove it.

Bleaching agents can be bought in the drugstore and will lighten hair that is darker than you are. The effect is not permanent. As soon as the hair grows out you'll have to do it again.

To remove hair yourself, you can either use a wax or a depilatory cream. The wax must be heated and spread over the hair. When it hardens, peel it off and the hair comes with it.

The depilatory creams are applied with a little stick to cover all the hair. Be sure and cover the hair because you can only do it once every twenty-four hours. Follow the directions on the package. Leave the cream on for a few minutes and then rinse it off. Don't leave it on too long because it can irritate your skin. When you rinse it off, don't rub. Some depilatories include a lubricant to put on afterwards. If yours doesn't, use Vaseline.

Depilatory creams can be irritating to your skin. Use only a cream that says it is all right for the face. It's also a good idea to test it on a piece of skin that is not ordinarily seen. The wax is a little messy but it can be reused and doesn't contain any chemicals. Whatever you use, follow all directions to the letter.

CHAPTER 3
Hands & Feet

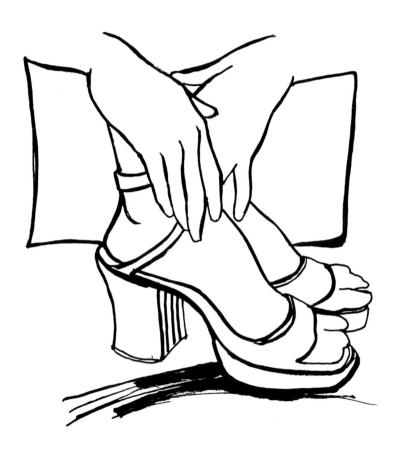

3

Your hands say a lot about you. Beautiful hands can be the finishing touch to a together look, but raggedy hands can be the one thing that destroys all your effort. Take care of your hands. Keep them soft and smooth and the nails healthy and well-groomed.

Because your hands are covered by a layer of very thin skin, they need lots of moisture. Apply lotion often during the day, especially after your hands have been in water. Massage the lotion into your hands by working from the wrist to the fingertips. This will help your circulation as well as moisturize your hands. For dry, chapped hands put a moisturizing cream (thicker than lotion) on before you go to bed and cover your hands with gloves. The heat generated works with the cream while you sleep. Use rubber gloves when you do chores that irritate your hands.

For well-groomed hands and healthy nails, a manicure once a week is a good bet. A manicure involves soaking your nails, removing old polish, filing, shaping and applying new polish. You'll need warm, soapy water to soak in, an *oily* polish remover and an emery board or even better a diamond nail file. Add an orangewood stick, a little cotton, base coat nailpolish, polish and top coat nailpolish. Now you're ready.

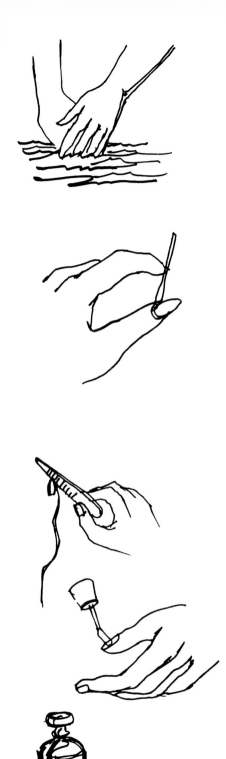

First, *remove all old polish.* Do this quickly since polish removers dry out nails.

Soak nails in warm, sudsy water for fifteen minutes. Dry thoroughly before filing.

Push cuticles back with orangewood stick wrapped in cotton. Cuticles are delicate, so do it gently. Push them back with towel every time you wash your hands.

File gently in one direction only. File from outside of nail to center on underside of nail. Use rough side of emery board to file and the other side to smooth edges. Nails should not be filed to a point. This causes them to break and split easily. Instead, make a soft, oval shape, following the curve of your finger tip.

Apply base coat or nail hardener if your nails are soft. Brush with even strokes from base of nail to edge. Allow to dry thoroughly.

Polish. 2 or 3 coats, but remember that polish must dry thoroughly before applying new coat. Wait about fifteen minutes between each application. Polish the same way as for base coat.

When nails are completely dry, put on top coat. This keeps polish from chipping. Dip your orange stick wrapped in cotton in polish remover and use it to remove any excess polish from around edges.

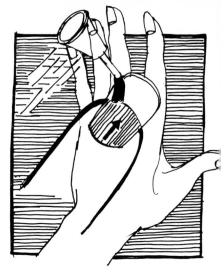

Protect your nails. Don't use them as if they're made of steel.

There are some common nail problems that can prevent your nails from being healthy and looking their best.

Brittle nails need moisture. Soak them in warm olive oil or baby oil before you go to bed. Also, don't use nail hardener or too much polish remover. Limit use of remover to once a week.

Soft nails can be made stronger by drinking more milk and getting more protein and oil in your diet. It's also a good idea to eat gelatin from time to time. It comes in several flavors and can be mixed with juice. You might want to use nail conditioners and hardeners. Put some under the nail as well for extra strength.

If you're a nail-biter, a weekly manicure can help solve your problem. File your nails short, to the tips of your fingers or even lower, as short as you can get them. There's less to bite that way. And once you're into the routine of giving yourself a manicure every week, your nails will look too pretty to bite. Nail polish tastes lousy anyway. Once you're pretty sure you've kicked the habit, you can grow your nails longer.

And how've your feet been treating you lately? Or better yet, how've you been treating them? For all the hard work they do for you and the long hours they put in on the job, they don't get nearly the praise they deserve. Do you let your feet know you love and understand them, or are you letting them go to the dogs?

Your feet need tender loving care just like the rest of you. That means soaking them, clipping the nails, using a pumice stone on rough spots, massaging them, exercising them and, most important, buying shoes that fit. Regular pedicures give your feet a neat appearance (keep this in mind during the summer when you're wearing sandals) and help prevent ingrown toenails, which are painful and a drag.

Soak your feet

You can buy a foot soak from the drugstore or you can use Epsom salt, which is really excellent. Even white vinegar makes a foot soak. All are to be mixed in warm water. If you're really desperate, just soak your feet in warm, sudsy water. Soak for 15 minutes. It will perk up your feet and soften the rough skin.

Clip your toenails

Do this right after the soak while your nails are still soft. It makes things a lot easier. Use toenail clippers. They're cheap, shaped especially for toenails and a lot safer than scissors. Clip them carefully, not too close, and straight across.

Don't forget the pumice stone

Rub it on the rough spots, particularly on the soles of your feet where callouses form. It's a good idea to use a pumice stone every day.

Moisturize

Moisturize your feet just as you would your hands. Rub in lotion from your ankles down to your toes, massaging as you rub. Also, don't forget those heels and soles.

If the shoe doesn't fit, don't wear it

The one most important factor in having healthy, good-looking feet is well-fitting shoes. If you constantly wear shoes that are too tight, too small or just plain uncomfortable, you will probably end up with callouses, corns and even bunions. All three of these afflictions are caused by ill-fitting shoes rubbing against different parts of your feet. The friction causes a

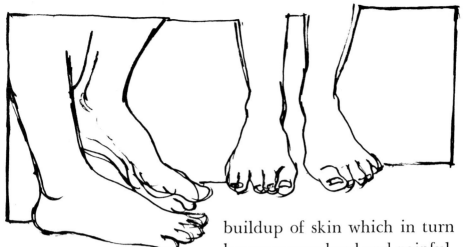

buildup of skin which in turn becomes very hard and painful.

Callouses are usually found on the soles of the feet and come from wearing shoes that are too high or that cause your foot to constantly slip down towards the toe of the shoe. The pumice will halt the growth of callouses if you catch them when they're just beginning. How can you tell? The sole of your foot will be sore.

Corns are also a buildup of layers of skin but they usually appear on your toes. These come from shoes that don't leave enough room for your toes to move. Again, it's the rubbing of the shoe against the toe that stimulates the corn to grow. They first appear as a red or tender spot that hurts whenever you wear the ill-fitting shoe. Once you discover what's happening, throw the shoes away or at least try not to wear them. If you keep the skin soft and don't wear the shoes that irritate that particular toe, the redness and soreness will go away and all will be well. Once a corn gets hard, it's there until a doctor removes it. Don't pick at it or cut it. You could do yourself a lot of harm. The same thing goes for callouses. It's better to soak and then pumice the dead skin off.

As for bunions, well, they're a bit more complicated than either corns or callouses. A bunion starts off as an inflamation of the fluid in a pocket between a bone or tendon in your foot. This little pocket is called a bursa. Eventually the bone itself becomes affected, begins to stick out and eventually will need corrective surgery. The only thing you can really do for bunions is stop wearing the shoes that are causing the problem and see a foot specialist.

Of course, there's a sure-fire way around all of this foot discomfort and that is to wear well-fitting shoes. Never buy shoes you can't try on first. Don't let eager shoe salesmen talk you into "breaking them in," either. Sure, leather does stretch—a little—but what are your feet going to do in the meantime? Try on *both* shoes with what you'll be wearing with them, that is, stockings or socks. Most people have one foot slightly larger than the other, usually less than half a size. But it's enough to make a difference. If the shoes are too hard to get on, forget them. Wiggle your toes. If you can't, then the shoe is not for your foot. Toes need room to breathe and relax. When you're standing up, there should be some space left between your big toe and the end of the shoe. Also, you know the shoe is too narrow if your little toe or the first knuckle above your big toe make the sides of the shoe stick out. On the other hand, shoes that are too big can cause your feet to slide around, again creating problems such as blisters and callouses. If shoes flop around too much on your feet, don't buy them.

Many women have a special problem—narrow heels. Most women's shoes are made to solve this problem. If, though, after you've tried on several brands, you find that you fit into a certain size but your heel slips up and down a bit, ask the shoe salesman to put in a small heel lift. This raises your foot up a fraction of an inch and often solves the problem.

It's worth spending a little more money to go to a reputable shoe store where the salespeople know how to fit shoes properly.

If you're having trouble finding shoes that fit, see a podiatrist. He'll be able to suggest a brand of shoe that's right for you and your particular feet. Most important, don't sacrifice comfort for style. Extreme styles like four-inch spike heels or platforms may go in and out of style, but your feet will suffer if you wear them. Stick to something more moderate. If you look hard enough, you can usually find something that's both comfortable and hip. When your feet hurt, the whole world knows it because it's written on every line of your face.

CHAPTER 4
Hair

4

Before we get down to styles and hair care, let's put to rest those old tired ideas about our hair. For just about as long as we've been here, black women have suffered behind their hair. We worried that it wasn't "good" or long or both. There's no such thing as good or bad hair. If someone is still trying to run that game on you, please set her straight. Hair can be in good shape, but that has absolutely nothing to do with how straight or long it is.

I grew up during the time when we went from being Nee-grows who hoped the world wouldn't notice to being black and proud of our heritage, our beauty and our race.

It's understandable, this thing about hair. For so long, all we saw was straight hair. Be it short or long, it had to be straight. If you weren't lucky enough to be born that way you had to spend the rest of your days in a never-ending battle of straightening combs, permanents, relaxers and anything that would promise straight hair. Well, we have finally arrived! Now you can walk down the street and see every possible example of black beauty. Big afros, close-cropped ones, cornrows, curls, straight, everything and anything.

So now we've broken out of that old good-hair/bad-hair bag, and I say right on to it! But we still can't relax about the care of our hair. That's just what happened when the afro came along. We'd spent all that time with chemicals and

heat and as soon as we adopted the 'fro we stopped everything. Hair got washed and maybe greased and that was that.
Little wonder our hair started falling out. There are a lot of
sisters today who will tell you they can't wear the afro because it makes their hair come out. That's because of the
way the hair was treated.

To have strong, healthy hair—no matter what the style—
you must take care of it. Washing and conditioning once a
week is a must. Oily hair needs to be washed more often than
that. Since oily skin and oily hair go hand in hand, if your
skin is oily you can bet your hair is, too. After all, your scalp
is an extension of your skin. Dirty hair encourages unhealthy
skin. Since many of us are strong on oiling scalps, we should
keep in mind that excess oil in hair acts like a magnet to
pick up all the dirt and grime that happens by. Shampoo
regularly. Here are some tips for the basic care of your hair:

49

The more you wash your hair, the gentler your shampoo should be

Lots of shampoos now have a little more to offer than just lather. Protein shampoos make the most sense since they reinforce the protein hair is made of. Herbal shampoos and shampoos with lemon smell wonderful. Balsam is a conditioner in itself besides smelling good, too.

Keep your hair out of hot water

Shampoo your hair in lukewarm or even cool water if you can stand it. Your hair doesn't need hot water to get clean. In fact, hot water and hot dryers take all the life out of hair.

Go easy on your hair

The ends of your hair are its most delicate part. That's because the hair shaft is completely exposed on the ends. The rest of the hair is protected by its own outer layer, but it too should be handled with care. Get your scalp clean but be gentle with your hair.

50

Be firm with your scalp

Massage your scalp with your fingertips as you wash your hair. Don't use your fingernails. Your scalp doesn't like to be gouged. A firm massage while washing helps stimulate circulation.

Condition with every shampoo

You have plenty to choose from. Some conditioners only take a minute while others can take up to a half hour. Most are to be put on after the shampoo. Some are combination setting lotions and conditioners and are not to be rinsed out. Read labels and follow instructions. When you rinse, use lots and lots of cool water to remove all traces of the conditioner. Conditioners penetrate the outer layer of your hair and make it smooth and easier to manage, but too much can make hair limp and without body. Homemade conditioners work just fine. A raw egg worked into hair and then rinsed completely out is an old standby. Try mayonnaise alone or with an egg. Overripe avocado is also good.

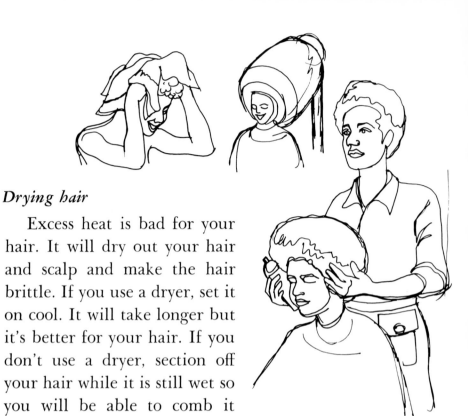

Drying hair

Excess heat is bad for your hair. It will dry out your hair and scalp and make the hair brittle. If you use a dryer, set it on cool. It will take longer but it's better for your hair. If you don't use a dryer, section off your hair while it is still wet so you will be able to comb it easily when it dries.

Now that your hair is all clean and healthy, it's time to think about a hair style. When you choose a hair style, it should be one that complements your facial structure. Hair does more for your face's appearance than any makeup tricks. It can make a fat face look thin or a long face look short.

Pull back your hair and check out the shape of your face. It's not the kind of thing that gets noticed for itself. You'll probably never hear the boys say, "Man, her face sho' got a fine shape," Learning how to pair it with the right hair style, however, is one of the basics to beauty. If you can't really decide what shape your face is, take an eyebrow pencil or lipstick and follow the outline of your face on the mirror. It won't be perfect, but it will give you a general idea. When you're drawing, follow the hair line.

Faces come in many shapes and sizes. There are oval faces, square ones, round ones, heart-shaped, oblong and pear-shaped, just to name a few. If your face is oval, consider yourself fortunate. You can wear any hair style you want. If yours is a square one, your hair should either be kept pretty short or be styled so it reaches below the jawline. Round faces need to look longer, so the sister who has one should concentrate on styles that are piled on top of the head. The heart-shaped face needs to be filled out around the jaws, so the hair style for that kind of face should be one that fluffs out at the ends and is fairly close to the head at the top. If your face is oblong and you don't want it to look any longer, stay away from hairdos that do just that. The small knots that have become popular have a tendency to make long faces look even longer. It's better to stick to the fuller, longer hair styles that are more flattering. The pear-shaped face needs to be filled out at the top rather than the jaw.

The way you part your hair is another way that you can make the shape of your face appear different. For instance, a center part works wonders on a round face to make it appear slimmer.

These shapes are general, of course. The best thing to do is experiment with different styles to find the best one for you. With the advent of the afro, the possibilities are really endless. You can get your afro shaped into the style that best suits your particular face. It is a good idea, though, to know what kind of face you have and what kind of style will be the most becoming to you. The only way you can possibly know this is to practice with various styles at home.

Any hair style is only as good as its cut. A good cut helps hair become stronger by exposing as little of the inside of the shaft as possible. That's where the protein and moisture are.

Having your hair cut straight across (a blunt cut) leaves less of the shaft exposed so less moisture and proteins are lost than if it were cut on an angle. A good haircut should flatter the shape of your face but allow freedom to change the style.

Hair should be trimmed fairly regularly to help control split ends. Otherwise, these damaged ends will break off and start the split over and over again. Split ends make hair hard to control and give the appearance of frizz. Also, because they continue the process of splitting and breaking, the hair doesn't get any longer.

Try to avoid rubber bands if you wear your hair up. They will break off your hair no matter how loose you wear them. Use bands specially coated for hair which are available at any five-and-dime store. To try the various styles that follow, you are going to need your own comb and brush, among other things. Keep these things clean and avoid using other people's.

When you wear the afro, it's pretty easy to get lazy about caring for your hair, especially if you're one of those lucky sisters who just has to wash it and leave it alone. It takes more than that to keep a nice bush, though. Washing and conditioning once a week is a must. Keep it well-oiled, too. Part your hair and oil your scalp. Then gently massage. This will stimulate your scalp and help to distribute the oil evenly. If your skin and hair are oily to begin with, skip the extra oil but massage your scalp with the tips of your fingers (not your fingernails!). Braiding helps, too, as long as you don't braid your hair too tightly. You could seriously damage the roots. Treat your hair like what it is, a part of your body. Nothing done to your hair should hurt. If your hair isn't really thick, braiding can make the ends straight and it will look a little messy the next day. If your hair is thick, though, braiding it is great. It makes your 'fro look fuller and makes it easy to manage.

When you pick your hair, be gentle. Picking can break it off. That's another reason to keep it well-conditioned and oiled. You won't have to pick it so hard because it won't be as tangled, so less will come out.

If you want to wear an afro but your hair is too straight or too fine to do it alone, you have two alternatives. One is to have it done professionally by way of a curly permanent. Most home permanents are straighteners and are not that strong. Remember, a permanent is just what it says: permanent! Not that it will last forever, but you'll have to live with it for several months whether you like it or not. Make sure you're sure before you go ahead with one. If your hair is in bad shape or it's been dyed, you should not use any kind of permanent or relaxer. So do it yourself—make your own 'fro.

For the do-it-yourself method you'll need lots of small rollers. The smaller they are, the kinkier the afro will be. You can find rollers made just for this purpose at some drug and variety stores. They're thin, made out of hard rubber and have their own rubber fasteners. If you use small sponge rollers, make sure you take your time removing them from your hair. They can be hard to take out and will break off very fine hair if you aren't careful. You'll also need end papers to keep the ends smooth and make rolling easier.

Roll your hair while it is wet. A combination conditioner/setting lotion comes in handy for this style. Part hair from side to side. Section off a very small amount of hair. Comb and then fold end paper in half the long way to cover end of hair. If hair is uneven, wrap paper closer to the scalp and then slide it to the end. Roll first roller to the right, second to the left, third to the right and so on until you have completed them all. Dry your hair at a cool setting.

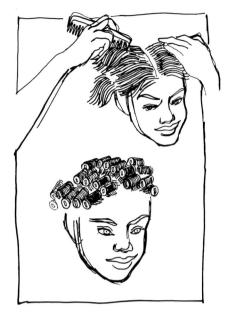

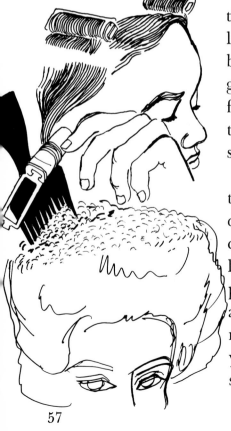

As you take rollers out, reroll the hair around your finger and leave it. When all rollers have been removed, pull curls apart gently with your fingers as you fluff with a pick. If the curls are too tight for you, work up a steam.

Turn the hot water on in the bathroom and close the door. The steam will loosen the curls. When you think they're loose enough, come out and pick again. Use your fingers along with the pick to fluff your new 'fro. When you have it as you want it, use *a little* hair spray to keep it in place.

You'll probably find, depending on the climate, that your new 'fro won't last too long. It gets pretty discouraging after all that work you put into it, but don't worry. If you keep it up, your hair will eventually get used to the idea and do it on its own.

As for sprays, no matter what they claim, they all build up in your hair and attract dirt like a vacuum. However, the awful truth is that we sometimes need them to keep stray hairs in place. When using hair spray, aim slightly *away* from hair and hold can about a foot away. This way only the mist will settle on your hair. If you use too much, your hair will feel sticky and look dull and dirty. Use it only when it's necessary and make sure and wash your hair often.

If you have hair that has been straightened by chemicals, you must take special care of it to make sure it doesn't fall out. Even the strongest hair in the world will fall out if mistreated. If you are thinking about getting a relaxer, remember, you'll have to do just as much to your hair as if you'd left it like it was. With a relaxer, it's rolling your hair tight that makes it straight instead of the pulling and heat of straightening combs. Relaxers and permanents also grow out. They have to be kept up regularly in order for you to keep a nice appearance. If you participate in a lot of sports, especially swimming, where your hair is exposed to chlorine, you're taking a risk with your hair. I would suggest an afro for the sports-minded sister. If you do decide on a relaxer, here are some things that will help keep your hair healthy and looking good.

Homemade conditioners really pay off. They are rich in moisture and will help keep hair nice and soft. Don't spend all your time concentrating on the scalp. Your hair is what really needs it.

Before you shampoo:
Dab slightly warmed olive oil on sectioned hair and hair ends with cotton balls. Wait five minutes, then shampoo.

or,

Mix one egg with about two tablespoons of mayonnaise. Cover all of hair, especially the ends. Gently work mixture into hair. Cover your hair with a plastic bag and sit under the dryer for ten minutes. Shampoo thoroughly.

After the shampoo, remove excess water. Use only enough cream rinse to untangle your hair. Rinse with lots of cool water.

If you use a straightening comb on your hair, make sure it's not too hot. When you press your hair with a comb that's too hot, the oil gets overheated and runs down the hair shaft into the roots. There it burns the delicate tissues. If this is allowed to happen every week, the damage will be permanent and baldness will set in. Once your hair starts falling out because of this, it doesn't grow back.

The ancient African art of cornrowing was brought here on the same ships that carried our ancestors to this country as slaves. It was quietly passed down through the generations until recent years when, because of a surge of interest in our African heritage and a need to recapture our roots, it rose to national prominence. Thanks to sisters like Cecily Tyson, who was one of the first black women to sport it with pride, cornrowing is taking its rightful place as a cultural institution.

Cornrowing is a continuous overhand braid that can be worn by all ages. Once you master it, you can create your own designs and styles. It can be dressed up by attaching beads or shells or ribbons, etc., or it can be totally casual. The styles are endless and it can take from a few minutes to all day to complete one.

HAIRSTYLES

PAGE BOY

A very simple, straight style for dressing up or dressing down.
It's great for all ages and super easy to do. Begin with
straight hair. Set it with big plastic curlers or heated curlers
in a high ring all around the crown; another ring of curlers
goes beneath the first ring if necessary. More than two rows of
curlers will make it too curly. If your hair is long enough,
you can set it with a single ring of huge curlers.

BIG 'BUSH'

Depending on its cut, the big afro can make your face appear
to be any shape you'd wish. It has even more versatility;
with a well-cut bigfro you can change your hair style in
a number of ways; the page boy style and corn rows can both
be done with the same basic cut.

SHORT AFRO

Closely cropped and neat, the short afro works well, is easy to care for and produces a sophisticated look.

CORN ROW I

For this simple style, part the hair from ear to ear. Make sure the parts are very straight. Then braid the front half forward and the back half down. To make the corn row braid, divide the beginning of the row at the crown into three small sections. Braid the first section, out and under. Each segment of the braid is picked up separately. You now pick up another section of hair about $\frac{1}{4}$ inch long, farther along the row,

and braid this in, again out and under as before. Continue
to the end of the row. Roll the ends under on small rollers or
pincurl them to finish off the look.

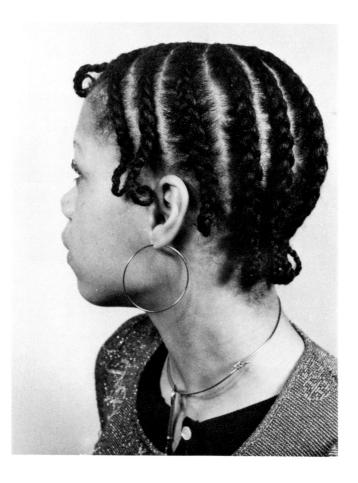

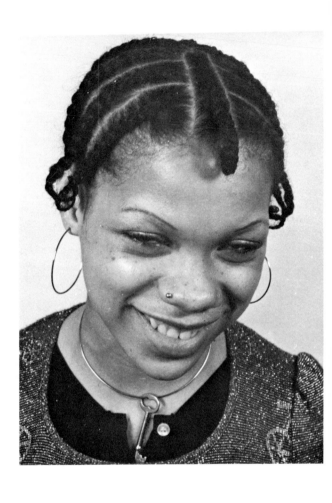

CORN ROW II

Begin at the top of the head. Part the hair with center braid
going forward and the rest going straight down. Braid, and
again, to finish this style, roll the ends under. Or dream up
your own style. Once you've mastered the parting and the
braiding, you can do anything with corn rows; you can even
spell out your name, if it's short enough, or at least your
initials. Corn rows can be combined with an afro for special
occasions; braid the front and leave the back in a bush.

68

Colorful wooden beads sewn into the end of each braid make the style elegant and pretty. It's probably best to enlist the aid of a friend while you're learning to braid corn rows, but once you're good at it, you can do your own.

CHAPTER 5
Health & Diet

5

Health and beauty go hand in hand. In fact, good health is the foundation on which all beauty is built. The way to good health is through eating the right foods, getting plenty of exercise and enough rest. When you're healthy, it shows on every part of you. Your skin is clear, your hair has life, your eyes shine and you have plenty of energy. In other words, you look good and feel good all over.

Energy is what makes your body run and all the energy you have comes from the food you eat. The only problem is that energy can't be tucked away for the future. Unused energy turns into fat. So eat just the amount your body needs to work its best, but make sure it does the work.

How much you need depends on a number of things. Height, age, build, amount of physical activity you do all have to do with how much you should eat and how much you should weigh. But because your body is still growing, there is no certain amount you should weigh, although a weight chart will give you an approximate idea about what's right for you. Even so, you should still be aware of what you're eating. That's where calories come in.

Calories are a way of measuring just how much energy you'll have when your body burns up food. By telling us how much energy we have stored, calories also tell us how much we need to spend to use them up. The more calories

we consume, the more exercise we need. Even though everything we do, even sleeping, uses some amount of calories, it's
really easy to take in more than we can use in one day. That's
when we get fat. The chart below gives an idea of how much
time it takes to work off certain foods.

VITAMIN	FOR WHAT	FOUND IN
A	hair eyes skin organs bones	liver yellow vegetables and fruits— (carrots, peaches apricots, sweet potatoes) green leafy vegetables

B_1	digestion	whole grain cereals
		liver, kidneys
B_2	nervous system	hearts
		milk
B_6	skin	vegetables
		fish
		eggs
B_{12}	eyes	nuts
C	skin teeth gums bones helps prevent colds or makes cold symptoms less severe	oranges lemons limes tomatoes green peppers berries raw cabbage liver green vegetables
D	teeth bones nerves	milk fortified with vitamin D fish livers
E	speeds up healing of scar tissue helps prevent scars from form- ing helps provide for more oxygen in your cells more available oxygen = more energy	egg yolk vegetable oils wheat germ oil whole grain cereals and breads
K	helps blood to clot	green, leafy vegetables yogurt

There must be a million different kinds of diets going around these days. All of them claim to be the one sure way to be beautiful and thin. They can really be dangerous because most of them limit what kinds of food you can eat and your body needs a variety. Besides, once you come off the diet and start eating a variety of foods, the weight comes right back. These fad diets are especially dangerous to girls in their teens because it's during those years your body is reaching full maturity. Unless it gets all the nutrients it needs, there could be serious problems later on. Also, if you don't eat the food your body needs, you'll become tired, lifeless and your looks will go down the drain. Eat for health and good looks, but do it sensibly.

Every body needs a certain amount of protein, carbohydrates, fats, vitamins and minerals each day to keep in good working order. The best way to get them is by eating the right foods. Fresh fruit, vegetables, fish, meat, poultry, bread, milk, cereals, etc., all provide you with the good things your body needs. (See charts.)

Don't get trapped by the super-vitamins. It's a fad these days to take massive doses of specific vitamins for specific problems, such as vitamin C for the common cold. Even though most vitamins are sold over-the-counter, it's a good idea to ask your doctor first if you think you need a particular vitamin in tablet form. Too much of some of these vitamins, just as too little, can cause problems. And the effects of massive doses of some of them are not known. The best way to get the nutrients your body needs to grow and stay healthy is to eat a balanced diet.

BASIC MINERALS	FOR WHAT	BEST FOUND IN
CALCIUM	bones teeth helps relax your nerves aid to sleep	milk mustard and turnip greens soybeans
MAGNESIUM	cell functions nerves	nuts soybeans green, leafy vegetables
IRON	rich, red blood	liver wheat germ eggs apricots molasses
IODINE	necessary for thyroid glands which affect growth, mental and physical activity	*iodized* salt
POTASSIUM	cell functions controls amount of water in your body (retention) helps send messages through nervous system	fruits vegetables meat nuts fish orange juice
SODIUM	cell functions water retention	table salt

CHLORINE	cell functions water retention makes hydrochloric acid in stomach, a digestive aid	table salt
PHOSPHOROUS	teeth, bones, cells	milk eggs cheese meats

When you eat is as important as what you eat. Don't skip meals. Your body needs fuel to run. Get it *before* you start rather than after you finish. Begin with breakfast. Breakfast should be your big meal and should include fruit or juice, cereal, an egg, toast and milk. Your body needs the most at the start of the day, but many of us do just the opposite: no breakfast, a light lunch and a big dinner. Lunch should be substantial. You're only halfway through the day, right? Dinner should be the lightest. Most of the day is over, so what do you need all that energy for? Sleep? When you eat, do it slowly. Try to get in foods from all the different categories. That makes for a well-balanced diet.

Of course, if you look in the mirror and see a fat tummy or old-age spread and you're not even twenty, then you know something should be done. And exercise is probably that something. If you are fat, though, you should see your doctor. He can tell if you need to be on a diet and will prescribe just the right one for you.

Bodies come in types. The type you are was determined by your genes way before you were born. Being fat is usually a combination of genetics and eating habits. Poor eating habits start at an early age, and once you have them it's hard

to change. You can have "fat" genes and still not be fat just by developing good eating habits.

Basic body types are the round, smooth ones, the athletic ones, with broad shoulders and narrow hips, and the tall, skinny, frail ones. Of course, there are combinations of these types, but usually one will stand out over the others. Whichever type you are, like it. Keep your body in the best possible shape and make it work for you. For instance, round and soft does not mean fat. Big can be beautiful, too. Develop a real friendship with your body. You can shape it up but you can't change it. A beautiful body, no matter what type it is, is one that's in the best condition. Here are some exercises that will help you get in shape and have a beautiful body, big or little.

Don't rely solely on an at-home exercise program to keep your body in shape. Any kind of exercise is good for you: sports, bicycling, dancing, running, and even walking. Some girls think that sports or any kind of vigorous physical exercise is unfeminine. They think that girls should be concerned only with dressing and making themselves attractive. Although those things are important, you can't be at your physical best unless your body is in good shape, and the best way to do that is through natural exercise. If you like a sport —basketball, tennis, softball, volleyball—participate in it. Make an effort to find some like-minded sisters and organize a team. You can get plenty of healthy exercise, for example, by playing one-on-one basketball, and you don't need a big team for that.

Swim in the summer. If you don't know how, take a course at your local YWCA. Swimming helps tone just about every muscle in your body. And walk anywhere you can—briskly. A fast walk is great for your legs and for your circulation. Try it. You'll feel better than if you rode a bus or a car. A walk in the light spring rain, if you're dressed for it, can make you feel romantic as well as exercising your body. If you go to a beach in the summer, take long walks in the sand. It takes some effort. You'll have to push hard against the sand with your toes. There's nothing better for toning your feet and legs. And if it's too far to walk, try riding a bike. It will do your thighs a world of good.

Some girls think that sports or any physical activity can cause bulgy muscles. Don't worry about it, it won't happen, unless you have a thing about weight lifting. The sports you play and the exercise you get can do nothing but firm up your muscles and keep you trim.

Posture is another thing to think about. Bad posture can make you look heavier than you are. And it's good for your body. If you learn to stand up straight now, your whole body will stay healthier as you grow older. A slouching girl never looks her best.

Wear a leotard or stand naked in front of a full-length mirror. Do your shoulders droop forward? Does your chin look mashed against your neck? Do your stomach and bottom hang out? Pull it all together and look better in minutes.

Stand with your feet together and parallel. Now pull your head up so the top of it faces the ceiling and your neck is extended, not falling into your shoulders. Pull your shoulders back and down, not painfully, just so they go straight across instead of drooping forward and so they don't look as if you're shrugging. Pull your hipbones up. This will flatten your stomach and tuck in your bottom. Align your legs so your knees are facing forward and your feet are parallel. There . . . don't you look better?

At first, standing up straight may seem awkward and uncomfortable. A lot of girls who develop big busts early get into the slouching habit to hide their breasts. And slouching is a hard habit to break. Try to be aware of how you're standing as often as you can, and make sure you're doing it correctly. In a while it will seem natural and comfortable, and you'll wonder why you ever started slouching in the first place.

Don't let good posture go when you're sitting down. Practice sitting in a straight-backed chair. Straighten your head and shoulders so that your whole spine rests against the back of the chair. Your shoulder blades should touch too. If you practice good posture you'll find that you move gracefully and look better all the time.

One last word—sleep. Make sure you get enough of it. Eight hours is about average, but some girls need more and some need less, so don't go by the clock alone. Sleep is important because it refreshes your body, gives it a chance to relax and renew itself. Enough sleep is important for almost everything you can think of. You'll catch fewer colds if you sleep enough. Your skin will be healthier with fewer blemishes. You'll avoid those baggy circles under your eyes. Sleep restores your body after the activities of the day. Give it a chance!

EXERCISES
For Your Stomach

Lie flat on floor. Stick your
feet under the sofa or bed
to hold them down. Clasp
hands behind your head.
Raise your body until your
elbows touch your knees.
Lower slowly to the count
of eight. Repeat five times.

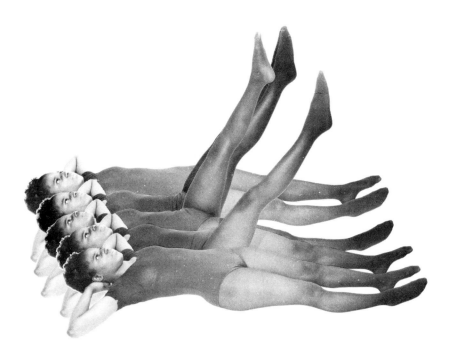

Lie flat on the floor with
both hands clasped behind
your head. Keeping your
legs straight, slowly raise
your right leg until it's
straight up. Lower it, change
to left leg. Now both, bring-
ing them down very slowly.
Repeat five times.

For Your Thighs

Bicycle

Lie flat on your back with your arms by your sides. Bring your knees to your chest. Place your hands under your hips and while straightening your legs, raise your hips off the floor until all of your weight rests on your head, shoulders and upper arms. Pedal your feet fifteen times.

Get down on your hands and knees. Bring your right knee up as you lower your head to meet it. Swing your leg out and up, keeping it straight as you lift your head at the same time. Repeat five times on each side.

For Your Hips

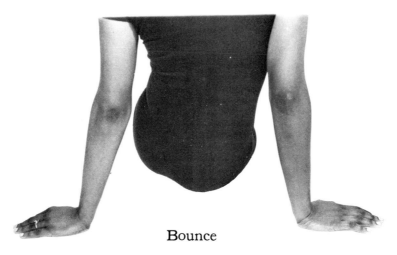

Bounce

Sit on floor with legs straight in front, arms at your sides. Lift your hips slightly from the floor, resting the weight on your hands. Bounce your hips on the floor five times each side. Then alternate from one side to the other.

Walks

Sit on the floor with legs together and arms straight in front. Pick up right hip and move forward. Keep doing this until you're "walking." Ten times forward and 10 times back.

87

For Your Waist

Sit on the floor with your legs spread apart. Holding your right ankle with your right hand, bend gently toward right foot. Return to center. Repeat for left side. Come to center with arms outstretched in front. Repeat five times each.

Toe Touch

Twist

Stand with feet slightly apart, hands on hips. Twist from the waist, keeping your hips facing front, first to the right, then left. Repeat 40 times.

A long time ago, menstruation was thought to be something dirty and awful. Actually, it's not a "curse" at all. It's a natural process that women's bodies go through each month. Each month your body builds up a supply of blood along the walls of the uterus. When the blood is not used to nourish a fertilized egg, it is discarded. Menstruation is the elimination of that blood. Because it's not needed, it just passes out of the body.

During this time you should take extra special care of yourself. Wash every day. There used to be a time when people thought you shouldn't bathe during menstruation, but now we know we can and *should*. As long as you make sure you don't get a chill, it's fine. Dry yourself off well. Also, make sure you change frequently whatever kind of sanitary protection you use. These things will help prevent odor.

Usually we learn from our mothers about personal hygiene and what kind of sanitary protection to use. It's more than likely whatever they're using. Of course, when our mothers were young girls napkins were the only thing available. There are many more things on the market now. Sanitary napkins come in many different shapes and sizes. There are sanitary panties and a variety of tampons. Frankly, there is no reason why young girls can't wear tampons. They are small and completely unnoticeable. But for girls with very heavy flows or bad cramps, sanitary napkins might be better, at least for the first couple of days. There are certain drawbacks to napkins, though. Sometimes you can see them if you wear pants, for instance. Because of their size, they are hard to carry around and dispose of and they can be uncomfortable. Finally, because they are worn externally, there's the problem of odor.

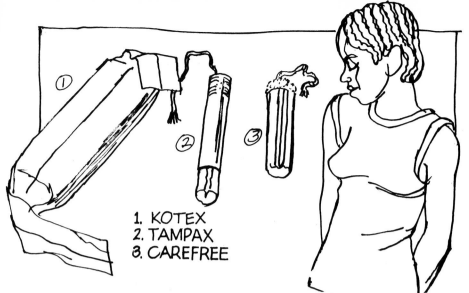

1. KOTEX
2. TAMPAX
3. CAREFREE

Tampons are good if your flow is not too heavy for them, but if you have bad cramps having something on the inside of you doesn't help. It may take a couple of tries before you can use a tampon, but the directions are easy to follow. Change it as often as you would change a napkin. Sometimes you might forget because you can't feel it at all.

If you have a heavy flow, you might consider wearing a sanitary panty along with whatever you use. This will protect you from staining your clothes.

As for activities, if your period is normal there's no reason why you can't go on with them just as usual. You can even swim if you wear tampons, but use the same rules as when you're bathing, that is, protect yourself from chills. I used to worry that the blood would flow into the bath water, but I found out the pressure of the water stops the flow. When you get out you should put on some kind of protection right away.

You may experience cramps of some sort or another. Cramps are caused by many things, from poor eating habits, to nerves, to the way you are built. You can't do much about the way you're built, but eating habits and nervous tension *can* be dealt with.

It's known that during the week before menstruation the amount of calcium in our blood drops to a low level. When there's not enough calcium in your blood, the muscles become irritable and cramps result. They can be in your legs and feet or, really, in any muscle. During menstruation, the low level of calcium results in cramps which can be easily cured by drinking lots of milk. Calcium tablets also can be taken for the pain. They are available in any drugstore. But since calcium needs vitamin D to work, they must be taken with milk, our best source of D. Surprisingly enough, those pre-menstrual "blues" come from the same thing—too little calcium. All of the irritability, nervousness and generally uncomfortable feeling can be prevented by increasing your calcium intake the week before your period begins and continuing it until your period is over. For severe cramps, though, that calcium doesn't seem to help, see your doctor.

Along with calcium, there are several other things you can do to make yourself more comfortable. The first thing is applying heat. Either wrap a hot water bottle in some towels or put a heating pad on your stomach. Heat will help relieve the discomfort. Another thing is to keep your hips higher than the rest of your body. This is done by placing pillows under your hips and feet. The lessened gravity slows down the flow and allows the blood to ease out around the clots. The second position is to get on your hands and knees with your hips up in the air and the top part of your body close to the bed. The same principle is at work here: gravity.

You may notice all kinds of funny things happening before your period begins. You might gain a few pounds. That's called water weight. Your stomach may bloat a little, but it's nothing to worry about. It will go away in a few days. You may feel depressed and irritable, too. At those times we're so into our sour state that we don't even consider what may be causing it. Now that you know calcium will help, just drink loads of milk and watch the blues fly out the window.

That doesn't mean you shouldn't do everything you can to make yourself feel better during these times. Pamper yourself. You deserve it.

Take a long, pink bath. And if it's possible, have your favorite music on, too.

Call your best friend and have a nice long chat.

Start a new book

Give yourself a facial or a manicure.

Think about all the things you love to do and do as many as you can. And cheer up! It won't last forever.

CHAPTER 6
The Clothes you wear

There's an old saying, "Clothes don't make the man."
Well, that holds true for women too, but while they don't
necessarily make you, clothes do say an awful lot about you.
Clothes are more than just a way to cover your naked body.
For centuries they have been used as a means of identifica-
tion. From soldiers' uniforms to the different kinds of habits
for different kinds of nuns, clothes have been used to state
a person's position within society. What you wear can iden-
tify you as a free spirit or a bit of a conservative—as a police-
man or a nurse, a pimp or a priest. What you wear says who
you are, what you do and, many times, how you think of
yourself.

Somewhere between the fig-leaf and the uniform, somebody decided to call it all fashion. It turned out to be a
pretty good idea too, since millions of women now wait with
bated breath for some strange person in some strange place
to tell them what they're going to be wearing six months
from today! And heaven forbid that you should want a red
dress when green has been declared THE color. But happily,
women are beginning to get hip and where fashion is concerned, are enjoying a much greater freedom.

When it comes to the difference between fashion and fad,
it's said that fashion is lasting while fads come one day and

are gone the next. Somehow all of this makes very little difference when you stop and think that the most fashionable phrase today is "do your own thing." When you shop, invest your money in clothes that make *you* feel good, not what's the whim of some fashion magazine.   Fad clothes go in and out of style very quickly, and it's easy to be left with a closet full of odd things that you never really liked in the first place.

There's something else that clothes can do beyond protecting your body and stating your position, and that is creating an illusion.

Have you ever noticed how black shoes make your feet look small while white shoes make them look large? Or maybe you're familiar with the question of which line is longer—this one or this one? $\longleftrightarrow$ $\succ\!\!—\!\!\prec$ They are equal in length. It's only an illusion that they seem different. Clothes work much the same way. Light colors make your body appear larger while dark colors make you look smaller. Vertical lines, lines that go up and down, give you a slimmer appearance and also make you look taller. Lines that go from side to side, horizontal lines, add the illusion of width and less height. It's a matter of how your eyes move. A white belt on a dark background attracts the eye and causes it to follow the horizontal line. A blouse tucked in a skirt gives your body a different look than an A-line dress. The skirt and blouse makes your eyes stop at the waist while the A-line of the dress makes your eyes go up and down.

Whether you're fashion-conscious, fad-crazy or fancy free, there are some basic rules about clothes and your body that never change. The first step is to KNOW YOUR BODY.

Take a good look in the mirror and decide, just as you did for your face, which areas could use a little help. It's about understanding how you are built and dressing in the way that's most becoming to your body. Now this doesn't mean if you're overweight you should only wear prison-striped muu muus. It just means that you learn how to bring out the best in yourself, and that's a good idea whether we're talking about makeup, clothes or even your personality, right?

Before you think about clothes, let's take a look at what you wear underneath them—panties, bras, slips, and pantyhose.

Panties these days come in many styles and fabrics, from old-fashioned cotton briefs to the skimpiest of lace bikinis. There are no rules to follow in your selection other than personal whim. Just make sure that your panties fit comfortably, that they don't bind at the waist or crotch. If you don't know what size to get, tell a saleswoman your skirt size and she'll be able to help you. A clean, soft pair of panties in your favorite color can make you feel pretty all day long.

Bras are something special. No two women have the same bosom, and fit becomes important. If your bra doesn't fit properly you may not be getting enough support or you may be damaging the tissue under your breasts, causing your bust to sag in a few years. Your bras should fit snugly for support, but they should not bind you or feel too tight.

The only way to be sure you get the right bra for you is to be fitted by a trained saleswoman. She knows what she's doing. She'll measure you and give you a wide selection of bras to choose from, and she'll make sure you get what you need. It's important to get help from her every time you need a new bra, even if you know your size. Different cuts fit entirely differently. It's not just your size, it's also your shape that has to be fitted. Being fitted each time is especially important if your bust is still growing. Also check your bra size if you lose or gain weight.

Not everyone needs to wear a bra. If you have small, firm breasts you may be better off without one. It's nice to have the free feeling that you get if you don't wear one, especially in the summer when each additional piece of clothing you wear makes you feel hotter.

The garter belt is a thing of the past. There's no need

to suffer stocking tops that show when you sit down. Pantyhose are here to stay. They come in all colors and many different weaves. Some stretch to fit several sizes. They are made for long legs, short legs, skinny legs, and fat legs. They go under anything—dresses, skirts, pants. The secret is finding a brand that fits you. Experiment with different brands, and once you find one that you like, stick to it.

Girdles are something you should stay away from while you're young. They may tuck you in temporarily, but if you wear one all the time your stomach muscles will become weak because the girdle is doing the work for them, and your stomach will stick out more than it did before. It's better to exercise and firm up your own muscles (see page 82). If you still think you need something extra to pull in your stomach, wear a light panty girdle or pantyhose with a support top. These will give you some control without damaging your muscles. To be on the safe side, though, try not to wear one except for special occasions or with a particular outfit.

A newer undergarment is the body stocking. It combines everything into one—bra, slip and panties. It fits like a leotard but gives you more support. And you only need to wear one thing under your dress or pants. Body stockings also come with legs attached, and with tank tops. You can pull yourself into one garment, put on shoes and skirt, and be ready to go.

For too long, fat sisters had to be out of style if they bought clothes to fit, but those days are over. Manufacturers are making just about everything in the larger sizes now. Of course, some clothes are designed for Twiggy types and no others, but if you're neat and your clothes fit well you should have few problems. When putting an outfit together one good rule is not to cut your body off in the middle. That means no contrasting color around your waist. Let the line your body makes be continuous. Dresses look better than blouses or body suits in skirts or pants, unless you wear some kind of top over them. That's cutting your body in half again. Vertical lines work well for you. In fact, anything that makes your eyes go up and down instead of sideways will work. Most important, buy clothes that fit *you*. No matter how your body is made, you should take pride in your appearance and concentrate on those clothes that look best on you.

Now we know that because light colors attract the light they make anything and anybody look larger. Dark colors repel light and therefore make you look smaller. Vertical lines lengthen your look while horizontal lines widen it. Those are the basic rules for color and line but there are other ideas that work for individual figure problems.

Height

If you want to look taller and slimmer wear outfits that are one continuous color, like all blue or all green in the same shade. It creates a vertical image that adds height and seems to trim off pounds.

If you think you're too tall or too thin concentrate on horizontal design and two-color outfits that shorten and widen the figure.

Legs

If your legs are *thin* and you'd like them to look larger, add a pair of white or light-colored pantyhose or tights.

Too *fat?* Dark panty hose will slim them down. Or if your problem is your thighs, you can stop the length of the skirt or dress right below them or try some of the nice knee length styles that are coming out.

Short legs can look longer if you keep your waist line high, wear one continuous color all the way to your feet and shorten your hem line.

Hips

If your problem is too much of a good thing, A-line dresses are an excellent way to camouflage them. If pants are your thing, it's a good idea to avoid pockets or anything else (low slung belts, for instance) that emphasize your hips. Also, a nice vertical stripe works wonders. In terms of color, your best bet is to stick with the darker shades and solids. Jackets that end at the hip line are another way of de-emphasizing your hips. Designs that draw the eye away from the hips are a good idea (like a way-out top) but remember, if you cut your figure in half by tucking it in you'll defeat your purpose. Generally, the one-color look is a better idea for the 'hippy' figure.

If you'd like your hips to look fuller, all you need to do is reverse the process. Light colored slacks, pockets, belts and prints will attract light and draw the eye to the hips. Tops tucked into slacks or skirts will also help emphasize this area.

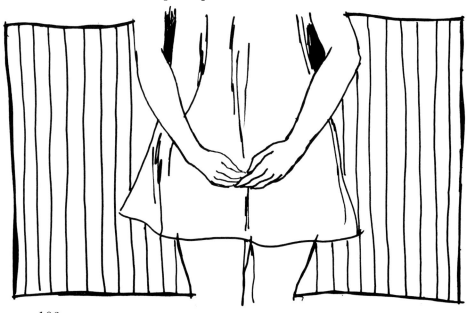

Waists

If your waist could stand to look *smaller*, avoid belts, tucked in tops and anything else that will cause the eye to stop there. Use one-color outfits to create the straight-line look from top to bottom.

For *short* or *high* waists wear your belts on your hip instead of at your waist line. Stick to the hip-hugging pants that add length to your torso. Also, the one-color dress is again a way of stretching your waist and the rest of you as well.

Tummy

If a fat tummy is your problem, the first thing to do is to avoid all tight fitting clothes. Wear tops on the outside of your pants or skirts that help to cover it up and give the appearance of a smooth line. Wear clothes with a slight fullness and don't cut your body off at the waist.

Bosom

Too small? Wear a top with lots of detail like ruffles or smocking, etc. Horizontal design will also give a fuller appearance to the bosom.

Too *large?* Avoid anything that's tight fitting. Jackets with small lapels take away from the large bosom. In terms of necklines, the V-neck and low-rounded ones draw the eye away from the bosom. It's a good idea to stay away from ruffles, horizontal stripes and any other frills that attract the eye and add extra fullness to an already full bosom. One-piece dresses that emphasize the vertical line also take away from the fuller bosom.

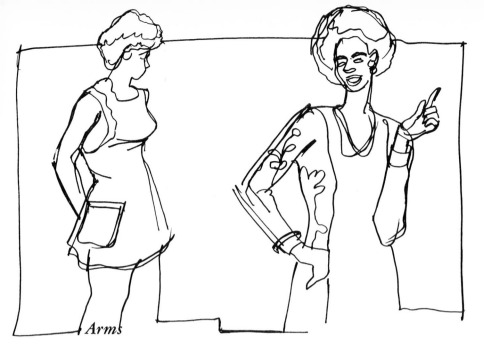

Arms

If your arms are too *large* you need to avoid sleeves that are too tight as well as sleeves that are too loose. Those that are softly shaped in between give the best effects. It's also a good idea to stay away from sleeves that are horizontally striped since they will only make large arms look larger.

If your arms are too *thin* to suit your tastes you should again avoid the extremes—too tight or too loose and choose instead the softer line in sleeves.

Shoulders

For shoulders that are too wide, stay away from padded shoulders and little puffed sleeves. Concentrate instead on sleeves that fall gently from the shoulder, jackets with narrow lapels and accessories such as long scarves or chains that emphasize the vertical line.

Puffed sleeves, padded shoulders, scooped-out necklines with simple sleeves widen the appearance of *narrow* shoulders.

Necks

The hairstyle you choose as well as clothes can solve the problem of a neck that is too *short* or too *fat*. Hair that's worn short or up will seem to add length to your neck as will V- or scooped out necklines. It's a good idea to avoid high, fancy collars and turtle necks.

These ideas will help your body to look more like you'd like it to, but keep in mind that it's really just an illusion and the *real* way to achieve the look you want is through proper diet and EXERCISE.

Being fashionable today is about finding the style that is YOU. Gone are the days when everything had to match. People are daring to throw plaids, prints, stripes and whatever else they can find together and what's coming out is the new individuality. Don't buy clothes you don't like or don't feel comfortable in just because somebody somewhere said you should. Clothes should reflect your personality and taste. Two women can wear the same dress and yet look totally different in it depending on how each of them chooses to define her own thing. Here's where accessories come in.

Shoes, hats, scarves, bracelets, handbags, gloves, necklaces, belts, pins—all of these things are accessories of one kind or another and all add the touch that not only reflects your personality but brings an entire look together. When choosing accessories it's a good idea to keep your wardrobe in mind and relate what you buy to what you already have. It's also important to note that accessories should complement your body as well as your clothes. The same rules of color and line that govern clothes also go for many accessories. For instance, say you've succeeded in finding the perfect one-color look. It's added height and trimmed off ten pounds. Then you throw a wide horizontally stripped belt across your middle. The whole look is blown. Size is important when you're choosing accessories. They shouldn't be too large or too small.

Developing a style or look is a very personal thing. Nobody can tell you the one secret to getting there because there isn't one. It does help though, to use your imagination and not be afraid to try something new.

When you're buying clothes, fit is everything. Different styles fit differently so don't be confused because you know you wear a nine but this nine is too small. Different manufacturers produce different sizes sometimes, and how a given dress is cut can make the difference. Types of fabrics also can make a difference in size. This is especially true when it comes to pants. Where something was made can also turn a nine into an eleven. Many clothes are made overseas and fit a little differently. Don't worry if you have one of every different size in the store in your closet. And don't worry if you have to move to the larger size. Those numbers don't mean anything and they don't show. What does show, though, is how you look in whatever it is you're wearing. In other words, buy clothes that fit YOU. If you can't try it on first, *don't buy it!* You can never be sure a thing will fit right until you do.

When you're trying on pants don't just stand and look. Walk, sit, bend, squat—do those things that you normally do. Pants need to be comfortable when you're sitting down just like when you're standing up. When it comes to jackets, coats, tops or dresses with sleeves, move your arms around and make sure to bend them at the elbow. Sleeves should be comfortable too, and nothing you buy should strain at the seams.

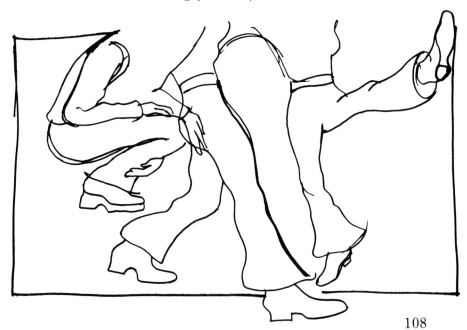

Besides look and fit there's something else to think about when you're buying clothes and that's how easy they are to care for. Today manufacturers are required to put instructions for care of their garments on the products themselves instead of on a tag that you can easily throw away. So when you're choosing something, look on the inside for instructions as to its care. With all the synthetics and blends, clothes are much easier to care for. Most things can be washed by hand and some can even be thrown into the washing machine. A few say machine dry as well, but unless you have your own dryer with different temperature settings I'd advise against it. There's no way to tell how hot commercial dryers are, so the safest thing to do is to hang it up to dry on its own. When washing by hand follow instructions for water temperature and gentleness. It does make a difference. Just as in machine washing, dark colors should be washed separately. If the instructions call for cold water use cold water. In other words, instructions are there for your convenience so follow them.

Sometimes things will shrink or fade when they're not supposed to, even if you follow the washing instructions on the garments. If this happens, note the manufacturer of the garment and switch to another brand. Once you find a few labels that are reliable and right for you stick with them as much as possible when you shop.

If you get a spot on your clothes your best bet is to take it to the dry cleaners. Tell them what was spilled on the garment. It'll make their job a lot easier and probably insure success. There are some spots though, that have home remedies. One of them is blood. If the garment can be put into water soak it immediately in *cold* water. Cold water soaks take out coffee, chocolate and wine too if you do it right away. Once it dries it needs professional help. Grease can be removed if you catch it before it's dry. Sprinkle any kind of talcum powder right on the spot. The powder draws the grease out of the fabric and after a few minutes it can be

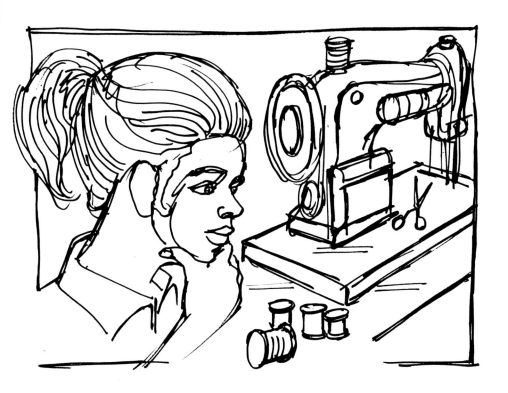

whisked away with whatever kind of brush you might have. Where your clothes are concerned there's no room for experimentation. If you don't know what the spot is, if it's something you're not sure about, or the garment says dry clean only, take it to the cleaners. Don't try to do it yourself. You just could make matters worse.

Aside from cleaning your clothes according to instructions, there are other ways you can care for them. Weed out your closet from time to time. Throw away your broken hangers, the shoes that are damaged beyond repair, etc. This will leave more room for the clothes you want to take care of. Think about what you have. If you have things that you never wear, that you don't really like, or that don't fit, give them away. Only keep the things you wear and like. If there's any mending to be done—hemming, putting on buttons, repairing a seam—do it as soon as you can and keep your clothes in circulation. Don't hang up anything that needs to be mended, cleaned, or washed. Do something about it first.

Dresses, skirts, and blouses should be kept on hangers. If you don't have a lot of closet space, get some hangers that can hold several garments at once. You may have some dresses or blouses made of delicate fabrics such as crepe. These should be protected by plastic garment bags against snags from other garments.

Jeans, T-shirts, and sweaters go in drawers or on shelves. They should be folded before you put them away so they won't get wrinkled. Underwear should also go in drawers. It's a good idea to put your clean pantyhose in plastic bags so they won't snag. Knitted dresses should also be folded and put in drawers. They can stretch and lose their shape if kept on hangers.

Don't forget your shoes and boots. Keep them in good repair. If they need heels or soles, get them before you wear them down further. They'll last longer if you keep them repaired and polished.

Your clothes are a reflection of your personality and say a lot about you. Choose them carefully and treat them well.